from notes of a troubled angel

Ridge Christian

BookLeaf
Publishing
India | USA | UK

from notes of a troubled angel © 2022 Ridge Christian

Presentation by *BookLeaf Publishing*

Web: www.bookleafpub.com

E-mail: info@bookleafpub.com

ISBN: 9789357444231

First edition 2022

DEDICATION

to Jordan, for making an angel out of me

to Rhonda and Mary, for giving me something I never knew I needed. Thank you

to Lola, an angel in the making

PREFACE

John 5:4

For an angel went down at a certain season into
the pool, and troubled the water: whosoever then
first after the troubling of the water stepped in
was made whole of whatsoever disease he had.

ENTER THE SERPENT

A stealthy and slippery villain,
with a tongue and wit as sharp
as the greatest warriors swords
Its hunger to deceive insatiable.

"Ah! a child of this God, let's see how righteous
your creations are."
The serpent slid up the tree to observe
the creatures who have been living in the garden.
He watched a man despair and relished in his
falling,
Until he watched a woman appear from his
body.
"How foolish are these beings? Blinded by this
holy fraud."

For weeks he has watched,
He knew with his help he could make them fall.
A delicious deceit.

Thin ice

Living on the edge of uncertainty
every step I take
eyes closed
i don't know when there will be
no more ground beneath
me

Line in the sand

I want to scream at you
until all I lose all the strength in
my vocal chords
There is so much rage inside me
because of you
You betrayed me at my hour of need
At the moment of truth, I trusted you
and you failed me
Why are you doing this to me?
Why are you taking my soul from me?

I want to scream at you
until I can't stop crying
There is so much sadness inside me
because of you
Just please stop breaking me
and hold me in your arms

exposed

when you finally see me
for what I am
it will destroy me when you leave
I'll try really hard for your love,
not good enough

sunbeam

I wish I could live in your warmth forever
In this moment you are my sun,
revolving around you I know what love is
open arms, I will bask in you because it gets
dark and frightening sometimes

Only you can burn the demons

catch me

why won't you give up on me
do you really think I'm worth saving
I want you to
afraid you'll regret it

The angel's keeper

Not good enough for heaven
but not wicked enough for hell
The angel is bound to his keeper
Another angel purer then he
The keeper knows of this angel
She has seen his rebellious actions towards the
father
and has seen his kindness towards the flesh
The angel is bruised for he's been marked
a mark of a vigilante
The keeper frowns at the sight of it
she thinks there is more to the angel than
defiance and autonomy
So she marks herself with the same
and tells the angel "there are now two of us,
angelic Adam and Eve. I have taken on your sin
and am no longer your keeper, instead your
lover."

No more today pt 1

Doesn't it get old
Sitting in your room
Drinking when you shouldn't be
Not making anything good
Are you a failure
Maybe
Isn't everyone?
Or do I want everyone to come down to my
level?

No more today pt 2

I feel so burnt out
Trying to express all these emotions
Sad, disappointed, angry
I spend most of my life alternating between
them
It's exhausting trying to be more than content
Because I find myself right back
Is this really what I am?
Am I just comfortable with this?
I feel as if my words that I write and say
get lost in an ocean of wasted time

Peace or madness by the Lake

I search for peace
out by the lake.
At 6:32 AM it is a silent sight to see,
the stillness of life and nature.
A beautiful sunrise to come soon with
the ripples of the water moving in a hypnotizing
rhythm.
Stillness of my heart is yet to be felt.

Before coming out to the lake, I took my coat to
battle the early morning chill.
Then came down the small hill to the dock to
find what I was searching for.
But what I found, at least at first isn't quite
surprising but still peculiar
I look at my reflection in the water.
All too familiar with.
I have eyes and nose and a mouth and a face,
but as I look closely, it's not really my face.
I practice smiling in the water.
The light behind my eyes and the cheeriness of
my smile has faded

away to weak and disappointing.

Then my reflection turned into an apparition of
what I used to be.
My moments of peace such as here by the lake
quickly turn me back to madness.
"Why don't I know you anymore?"
I am tired.
My teardrops breaking the image in the cold
morning February water.
I wish I could be that old apparition
and drift away in the calm ripples.

Ballad of the Lovesick

While you're sleeping
next to me
I look at our pictures
as if I lost it all.
It's all in my head.
I've never known a feeling
this great so
it must be destined to end.
Then you roll over and whisper,
I figure it's sleep speak
the whisper comes again
I answer the call
I lie down
she opens her eyes,
suddenly I'm all alone

torch

I'm running away
so I feel like burning every bridge
This place has defeated me
I burnt my home to the ground
and told my friends I was leaving and never to
return

I gave them the ashes from my home
I told them to remember me in the flames
When I was bright and full of passion
and mourn for me in the ashes

black square

the ceiling mocks me every night
never saying anything nice
it doesn't say anything to
me at all really
much like the people I love
because I'm always the reason

parking lot
fellowship

I'm much more content
sobbing in a church parking lot
that I found on the side of the road
in West Virginia
than having to deal
with greatness I blew

jaded

I am afraid of you and someone like you
there is no more honor in vulnerability
only shame and broken spirits

Job's interlude

I remember when I was walking with the
demons
They were ugly creatures but some looked like
you and me
This isn't my first time walking with them
It happens so much at this point one would
consider us friends
They are always trying to deceive me
In time, I will know sacrifice
I will know pain, suffering
but in the end you will know what it's like to
lose
Faith is the flame to the devil's icy grip

Envy

I was on my phone one day scrolling in the
digital abyss of faces on a screen
Something stopped me
A post of someones successes
Accolades and oppurtunities that sounded too
good to be true
Jealously rising like an explosion in a well
I can't wait to crawl under my blanket and curse
you in private
then see you in public and look into your eyes
and hope for your demise
I walk away weaker than a shattered dream

the angel that came to John (Revelation)

I was born
but I do not exist
Throw me into the sun and see if I burn
Plunge me into the ice and see if I freeze
I am the angel of old
I was there with the shepherds and the serpent
In time the Lost City will rise and wicked will
be slain
I will be there again and you will ascend with
the angels